ISBN 978-1-332-15066-3
PIBN 10291475

1 MONTH OF
FREE
READING

at
www.ForgottenBooks.com

By purchasing this book you are eligible for one month membership to ForgottenBooks.com, giving you unlimited access to our entire collection of over 700,000 titles via our web site and mobile apps.

To claim your free month visit:
www.forgottenbooks.com/free291475

THE

" Deepest mouthed against the Government."
Dryden.

STRONACH, GEORGE

THE LIBERAL

MIS-LEADERS.

"THE QUEEN HATH BEST SUCCESS WHEN YOU ARE ABSENT."

3rd Henry VI.

WILLIAM BLACKWOOD & SONS

EDINBURGH AND LONDON

" Saul may have slain his thousands, and David his tens of thousands, but each has done a hero's part, and every one of the late Ministers may claim a share in the diminution of the Liberal ranks."

Joseph Chamberlain, M.P.

Preface.

The late PRINCE CONSORT *to* LORD ABERDEEN.

"ANY such declaration as Mr Gladstone has made on Mr Disraeli's motion on the Crimean War must not only weaken us abroad in public estimation, and give a wrong opinion as to the determination to support the QUEEN in the war in which she has been involved, but renders all chance of obtaining honourable peace without great fresh sacrifices of blood and treasure impossible, by giving *new hopes and spirit to the enemy.*"

"If a house be divided against itself that house cannot stand."

"Its all very well to talk, but acting's a different thing."
Dickens.

𝕲𝖑𝖆𝖉𝖘𝖙𝖔𝖓𝖊 𝖙𝖍𝖊 𝕲𝖗𝖊𝖆𝖙.

"Mr Gladstone's measures have reduced the great and glorious Empire of which he was put in charge to a manufactory of cotton cloth and a market for cheap goods, with an army and navy reduced by paltry savings to a standard of weakness and inefficiency. By his foreign policy Mr Gladstone has tarnished the national honour, injured the national interests, and lowered the national character."

LORD JOHN RUSSELL.

"Whatever Mr Gladstone sees is refracted and distorted by a false medium of passions and prejudices. The more strictly Mr Gladstone reasons on his premises, the more absurd are the conclusions which he brings out."—*Lord Macaulay.*

"Alexander II., who has achieved for Russia its noblest and most enduring triumphs." *W. E. Gladstone, M.P.*

"Nature teaches beasts to know their friends."
Coriolanus.

"Lord Hartington,—the serious son of a respectable Duke."
Joseph Chamberlain, M.P.

Haughty Hartington.

WANTED.

A LEADER for the Liberal Party.

Apply at the Reform Club.

WANTED.

A PARTY for the Liberal Leader.

Apply at Devonshire House.

"No young divine, new beneficed, can be
More pert, more proud, more prejudiced than he."
Pope.

"Dux—*et præterea nihil.*"

"As the prompters breathe, the puppet speaks."

Pope.

"I'm a Quaker, sly and dry."
Lord Neaves

Mr Bright's Opinion of the Church.

"The Church is always on the side of the Tory Party. Be it in town or be it in country—you will find that the Church is never a centre of political light, but of political darkness."

JOHN BRIGHT, *25th January 1875.*

"The Chancellor of the Duchy of Lancaster (Mr Bright), being a Quaker, resigned the duties of Military Paymaster to somebody else, and gave up the only thing which he was required to do, except draw his salary."

"Let Ireland work out its own redemption."
John Bright, September 1848.

"When a man is in office he is not the same man as when he is in opposition." *John Bright, M.P.*

"Peace—at any price."
(*With apologies to* Mr PUNCH.)

"Mr Bright has been deposed from the high rank of a destructive spirit to the inferior grade of a guardian angel."

Sir William Vernon-Harcourt, M.P.

"My policy is myself."
Swift.

Mr Lowe on the Working Man.

I.

"We know what sort of persons live in small houses; we have had all experience of them under the name of 'freemen,' and it would be a good thing if they were disenfranchised altogether."

Mr Lowe, *Speech on the Reform Bill, 1866.*

II.

In June 1873, the "*Times*" recorded that Mr Lowe and his bicycle ran over a working man, that Mr Lowe refused to pay the doctor's bill, and that his victim, giving way to melancholy, eventually committed suicide.

"Full of the milk of human kindness."
Cymbeline.

" He treats everybody who happens to differ from him either as a fool
r a knave."—*Sheridan.*

" Beauty, wisdom, modesty."
Merchant of Venice.

" It would be interesting to know how many supporters were irrecover-
bly lost by Mr Lowe's successive Budgets."—*Joseph Chamberlain, M.P.*

𝕷𝖔𝖗𝖉 𝕲𝖗𝖆𝖓𝖛𝖎𝖑𝖑𝖊

ON THE

DISMEMBERMENT OF THE EMPIRE.

" Many thoughtful men and statesmen, after deeply meditating the subject, have come to the conclusion that a perfectly friendly separation should take place between England and Canada."

LORD GRANVILLE, 14*th February* 1870.

" Do nothing, and nothing comes of it; let things drift, and sooner or later they will come to an anchor."

" Some that smile have in their hearts, I fear,
Millions of mischief."
Julius Cæsar.

" *Oui, Messieurs.*"

" The thing has travelled, speaks each language, too,
And knows what's fit for every State to do."
Pope.

"Should pride expect to 'scape rebuke
Because its owner is a Duke?"

Swift.

"The Master-Fiend Argyll!"

W. E. Aytoun.

"As to the Duke of Argyll's violent charges of misrepresentation and falsehood, it may be sufficient to say that a speaker who advances such accusations should come forward with clean hands, and he himself indulges in misrepresentation which, if his example were to be followed, might well be characterised in his own terms."

The " Times."

●

"Hark! hark! I hear the strain of strutting chanticleer
Cry, Cock-a-doodle do!" *The Tempest.*

"A fiery soul, which, working out its way,
Fretted the pigmy body to decay."
Dryden.

" Besides, his memory decays,
He recollects not what he says."
Hudibras.

Cheese-paring Childers.

" Enough has transpired to show that from undue economy, or negligence, or simple stupidity, a vessel was sent to sea under conditions which filled people at the time with apprehension that the warnings given to the Admiralty were disregarded, and that there is good reason for supposing the disaster to be the direct and almost necessary consequence of the state of the ship."

The " Times" on the " Megæra" Blunder.

" A very conscientious Minister, because he was at sea from the hour of his appointment till the hour he resigned."

" And did not guide the man-of-war."
Hudibras.

"Ships that have gone down at sea
When heaven was all tranquillity."

Moore.

"The English fleet thou canst not see—
Because—it's not in sight."

Sheridan.

"Methinks I am a prophet!"
Richard II.

"The Political Zadkiel."

"The hon. and learned Member for Oxford appears to emulate the fame of "*Zadkiel's Almanac*," and is in the habit of giving a very large number of prophecies each year, assuring us that all previous prophecies have come true."

SIR STAFFORD NORTHCOTE, M.P.

"I have but one fault with the hon. and learned Member for Oxford (Mr Vernon Harcourt)—he thinks all the world is as clever as himself."

MR LOWE, *1st May 1871.*

"He accepted office under a Ministry he had previously opposed in every possible manner."

"*Saturday Review.*"

"Neither, gentlemen, am I come to Birmingham to prophesy. Inspiration only comes to me on my domestic tripod."

Sir William Vernon Harcourt, M.P.

"Really his utterances, are they not a kind of revelation?"
Carlyle.

"The Right Hon. Gentleman is indebted to his memory for his jests, and to his imagination for his facts." *Sheridan.*

Watery Wilfrid.

" Pray, what's this ' Local Option ' Bill.
That some folks rave about?
I can't, with all my pains and skill,
Its meaning quite make out.
O! it's a little simple Bill
That seeks to pass *incog.,*
To *permit* ME—to *prevent* YOU—
From having a glass of grog.' "
LORD NEAVES' *"Songs and Verses."*

" Another set of gentlemen, represented by Sir Wilfrid Lawson
and the United Kingdom Alliance, think that, because *they* prefer
water, the very essence of Liberalism consists in making it practically
impossible for a man, unless he has a cellar of his own, to get himself a glass of beer." *Lord Derby, 17th Dec. 1875.*

"Dost know this water-fly?"
Hamlet.

"Example is better than precept."

"I will make it felony to drink small beer."
2nd Henry VI.

Sir Citizen Dilke.

" He is unhappy when dealing with facts. He asserts that the Queen's pages do not pass examinations when they enter the army, whereas they pass examinations. He asserts that the Queen pays no income tax on her income, whereas she does pay it. He asserts that the appropriation of savings out of the sums voted by Parliament from the Civil List to the Privy Purse is directly in the teeth of the Act of Parliament, whereas the Act expressly authorises such an appropriation. Nevertheless, upon such inventions he has founded a suggestion, so presented, that it almost amounts to a charge of conspiracy between Her Majesty and the Treasury to form a large private Royal fortune in an unlawful manner."   "*Vanity Fair.*"

"LICENCE they mean when they cry LIBERTY."
                                        Milton.

"A hot-headed young man."

John Bright, M.P.

"From all men thou art emancipated but from thyself and from the devil—and thou pratest of thy liberty ! thou entire block-head."

Carlyle.

"He rose like a rocket, he fell like the stick."
Tom Paine.

Derby the Deserter.

"I am not equally sure that I do know what Liberalism—in the party sense, the Liberalism of the great Liberal connection—is supposed to imply. The name was a very happy one, whoever hit upon it—because, according to the construction the speaker puts upon it, it may signify anything or nothing."

LORD DERBY, 1875.

"Still violent, whatever cause he took,
But most against the party he forsook,
For renegadoes who ne'er turn by halves
Are bound in conscience to be double knaves."
Dryden.

"The coward that would not dare."
Sir Walter Scott.

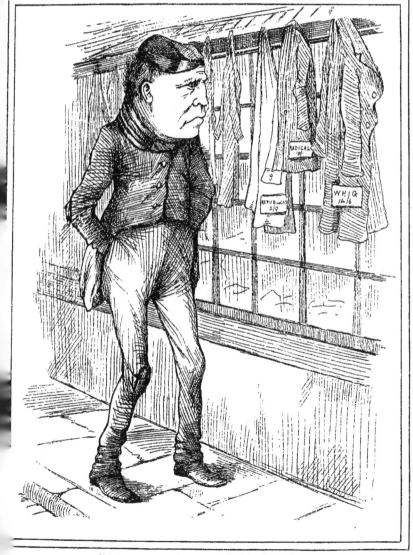

"I leave my character behind me."
Sheridan

"Brave undertakers to restore,
That could not keep yourselves in power."
Hudibras.

"The Ministry of all the virtues and untaxed trumpets."

"𝕎olbes without a Shepherd."

Sir Robert Peel.

"A motley horde of *moblots* and *franc-tireurs*, held together by nothing but a common animosity."

"Mr Gladstone's Government fell because nearly every member had made himself personally odious, and the people of England were determined to have nothing to do with them any longer."

PROFESSOR THOROLD ROGERS,
Liberal Candidate for Southwark.

"Next these a troop of busy spirits press,
Of little fortunes, and of conscience less."
Dryden.

"Such as cannot rule, nor even will be ruled."
Coriolanus.

"Alliance with one is apt to be estrangement from another."
W. E. Forster, M.P.

PLAICE FISHING.
"Put the puppets in the box, for the play is played out."
Thackeray.

" Whip me such honest knaves."
                        Othello.

" Th' offending ADAM."
                        King Henry V.

"The best of prophets of the Future is—the Past."
Byron.

"At a moment's notice the dissolution was re-solved on, and Mr Gladstone promulgated through the country the meanest public document that has ever, in like circumstances, proceeded from a States-man of the first rank. His manifesto was simply an appeal to the selfishness of the middle classes. Nearly two columns of the *"Times"* were filled with a sketch Budget and the promise of the repeal of the Income Tax, while ten lines were thought sufficient for the statement that changes might *possibly* be found desirable in the Franchise, the Land Laws, the Game Laws, the Education Act, the Licensing Laws, and the acts affecting Trades' Unions."

JOSEPH CHAMBERLAIN, M.P., *October* 1874.

THE GENERAL ELECTION.

CPSIA information can be obtained
at www.ICGtesting.com
Printed in the USA
BVHW040918211218
536170BV00015B/548/P